HOW TO IMPROVE AT
DRAWING

Sue McMillan

 Crabtree Publishing Company
www.crabtreebooks.com

Author: Sue McMillan
Editor: Adrianna Morganelli
Editorial director: Kathy Middleton
Prepress technician: Margaret Amy Salter
Production coordinator: Margaret Amy Salter

Photo credits:

Copyright © Paul Bryn Davies: pages 38–45

Getty Images: AFP: page 4 (top); Peter Mason: front
cover; O. Louis Mazzatenta: page 4 (bottom);
Tim & Life Pictures: page 5 (bottom)

Copyright © Susie Hodge: pages 28–31

iStock: page 4 (middle), page 5 (top)

Superstock: Joseph Barnell: page 46 (bottom);
Bridgeman Art Library, London: pages
5 (middle), page 46 (top)

Musee d'Orsay, Paris, France/Giraudon/
The Bridgeman Art Library: page 47 (top)

M.C. Escher's "Drawing Hands" © 2009
The M.C. Escher Company-Holland: page
47 (bottom)

All other photographs copyright © Search Press Ltd.

Library and Archives Canada Cataloguing in Publication

McMillan, Sue, 1973-
How to improve at drawing / Sue McMillan.

(How to improve at--)
Includes index.
ISBN 978-0-7787-3576-2 (bound).--ISBN 978-0-7787-3598-4 (pbk.)

1. Drawing--Technique--Juvenile literature.
I. Title. II. Series: How to improve at--

NC655.M367 2010   j741.2   C2009-907052-9

Library of Congress Cataloging-in-Publication Data

McMillan, Sue, 1973-
How to improve at drawing / Sue McMillan.
p. cm. -- (How to improve at--)
Includes index.
ISBN 978-0-7787-3598-4 (pbk. : alk. paper) -- ISBN 978-0-7787-3576-2
(reinforced library binding : alk. paper)
1. Drawing--Technique--Juvenile literature. I. Title. II. Series.

NC655.M38 2010
741.2--dc22
                                           2009049079

Crabtree Publishing Company

www.crabtreebooks.com   1-800-387-7650

Published in Canada
Crabtree Publishing
616 Welland Ave.
St. Catharines, Ontario
L2M 5V6

Published in the United States
Crabtree Publishing
PMB 59051
350 Fifth Avenue, 59th Floor
New York, New York 10118

Printed in the U.S.A./012010/BG20091216

CONTENTS

• INTRODUCTION   3

• KNOW THE CRAFT
A History of Drawing   4
Equipment   6

• TECHNIQUE
Perspective and Observation   8
Tone, Texture, and Color   10
Composition   12
Water and Sky   14

• FLORA AND FAUNA
Flowers   16
Birds   20
Cats   24
Dogs   28
Horses   32

• FOLKLORE
Leprechauns   36
Fairies   38
Dragons   42

• SOME FAMOUS ARTISTS   46

• GLOSSARY & INDEX   48

2

INTRODUCTION

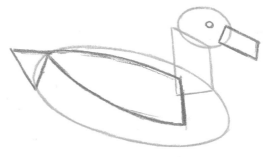

Drawing is an art form that has been around for thousands of years. Since prehistoric times, when humans made their very first marks on the walls of caves, people have wanted to record what they see around them as drawings and paintings. Drawing can appear challenging to the beginner, but in this book you will find all the advice on basic equipment and techniques that you will need.

DRAWING ON EXPERIENCE

In order to draw realistic pictures, you need to develop your powers of observation. Spend some time every day looking at a landscape or an animal. Look at light and shadows, and focus on any interesting shapes or textures.

Get in to the habit of carrying a small sketchpad and a pencil with you. Whenever you see something interesting, you can do some quick sketches. If you have one, a camera will help you capture an image to draw in more detail. This is very useful when you are observing animal **subjects**. Remember—the more you draw, the better you will become!

GUIDE TO STEPS

In this book, we will show you step-by-step how to draw everything from cuddly cats to fierce dragons.

You will see how to break images down into manageable steps, starting with basic geometric shapes to build the outline of your subject. Each step shows new lines in a different color than in previous steps. Once you have mastered these examples, you can use the techniques to sketch just about anything!

A HISTORY OF DRAWING

For thousands of years, people have experimented with anything they could find in the world around them to draw or paint. Artists have used every kind of material and technique, from wood to plaster, and canvas to the computer.

CAVE PAINTINGS

In some of the earliest known drawings dating from prehistoric times, humans painted scenes on the walls of caves deep underground. Many examples survive today. One of the best-known, in Lascaux, France, shows images of animals, such as this bull (right), humans, and abstract symbols.

ANCIENT EGYPTIANS

The ancient Egyptians drew detailed scenes of the afterlife on tomb walls. In Egyptian art, people were always drawn in profile (from the side). Carved picture symbols called hieroglyphs were also used to describe the scenes (left). A very important development in the history of drawing was the Egyptian invention of papyrus—a paper produced from the papyrus plant.

ANCIENT GREEKS

The ancient Greeks added landscape and detail to their wall frescoes, or paintings (right). Smaller works, or panel pieces, were painted onto wooden boards. Sadly no panel paintings have survived, and few examples of the frescoes have survived the last two thousand years undamaged.

ANCIENT ROMANS

Architectural scenes, landscapes, and scenes from mythology were the most popular subjects for the ancient Romans. They added detail to their landscapes, and tried to give drawings a sense of **depth**. They improved texture and **shading**, but there were still problems with scale. Most of the surviving examples of artwork from this period are preserved as frescoes like this one in Herculaneum, Italy.

THE RENAISSANCE

From the twelfth century, when paper became more widely available, artists began to use paper to plan paintings by first sketching out their ideas, instead of sketching them straight onto the walls or canvas, then covering them in paint. Many examples of sketches have survived. The most well-known are those by Italian artists Leonardo da Vinci, Michelangelo, and Raphael, whose fresco (left) is in the Vatican in Rome. With so many impressive artists producing exceptional works, drawing took off as a separate form of art.

THE PRESENT DAY

Over the centuries, drawing has continued to develop as an art form, with many artists using sketching to experiment and develop their techniques. Some of the most renowned twentieth-century artists, such as Goya, Klee, and Kandinsky, have used line work to create amazing pieces. Works like this drawing of a ballerina by the French artist Degas have confirmed drawing as a distinct art form. Today, for some artists, a screen has replaced paper, and a stylus or mouse has replaced the pencil. The drive to create and make a mark, however, is as strong today as it was in prehistoric times.

EQUIPMENT

Art materials can be expensive, but you may have some of the basics at home. Large stationery stores will carry a simple range, but for specialty items, an art shop is best. You can also order goods through catalogs or the Internet, but the downside to this is that you cannot try before you buy.

PENCILS

The pencil is one of the most flexible pieces of art equipment. Work can be rubbed out fairly easily, so you can experiment with confidence. Graphite pencils are graded by their softness, and range from the hardest, 9H, to the softest, 9B. Softer pencils tend to **smudge** easily, so they are great for shading.

For the beginner, it is best to start with mid-range pencils, such as HB, 2B, and 4B. Then you can experiment with others as your confidence grows.

PAPER

Paper comes in a variety of colors, sizes, weights, and textures. Choosing your drawing surface is a personal choice, but most artists prefer to use paper with a weight of 65 pounds. **Sketchbooks** are an obvious choice, and a small letter-sized pad is ideal for carrying around. For larger works, choose a legal- or ledger-sized pad. Ordinary blank paper is a good cheap option, or larger sheets that can be cut into smaller pieces. The most economical way to experiment is to use scrap paper, such as old envelopes, wallpaper scraps, or even scrap cardboard.

STUMP

A **stump**, or torchon, is a pointed stick that is made from tightly rolled paper fiber. It is used for **blending**. However, a clean, soft rag wrapped around a finger or a cotton swab will also work.

WEDGE ERASER

Wedge erasers can be used to blend or lighten your drawing, as well as to rub out mistakes. Pencil-top wedge erasers are the perfect choice and are easy to use.

SPRAY FIXATIVE

Spray **fixative** is the most convenient way to "set" pencil drawings. Apply it in a mist of several thin layers, vertically then horizontally. Allow time to dry. It is wise to practice on an old sketch first to ensure that you do not apply it too thickly. Always use fixative in a well-ventilated room.

OTHER EQUIPMENT

COTTON SWABS—Useful for fine blending, especially with charcoal.

CRAFT KNIFE—An effective tool for sharpening pencils and crayons. It can also be used to scratch minor details into pictures, although care must be taken not to damage the paper.

INK ERASER—The easiest eraser to use on ink is a tool with an eraser at one end and a brush at the other. Used carefully in emergencies, this can be a great help.

PUTTY ERASER—A versatile piece of drawing equipment, as it can be squeezed into any shape. As well as correcting mistakes, it can also add **highlights**, be pressed down to lighten shading, and be rolled to a point to remove tiny mistakes.

SANDPAPER—Medium-grade sandpaper is ideal for keeping a sharp point on your pencils.

STICKY NOTES—When you need to do hard erasing, these can be used to mask your drawing.

TISSUES—If you do not have a stump, cover your finger with a tissue to avoid rubbing acid into your drawing. Avoid blending with a bare finger.

PERSPECTIVE AND OBSERVATION

Perspective can be a confusing concept at first, but in order to draw accurately, it is an important technical skill to master. Knowing the simple rules will give a sense of depth and realism to your drawings. Once you understand the basics, study famous works of art to see how perspective has been used. It may surprise you to see that art that seems very loosely painted—like the waterlilies by French impressionist Claude Monet—still has perfect perspective.

EYE LEVEL

Finding the eye level, or horizon, on a corner, such as on a brick building, is easy. Hold a pencil horizontally at arm's length over the corner. Keeping one eye closed, move your pencil down the corner. The eye level is the point where the lines made by the bricks on each side of the corner meet to form a horizontal line at the top edge of your pencil. You can use the same technique with photos by placing your pencil horizontally on the picture and moving it up and down.

VANISHING POINTS

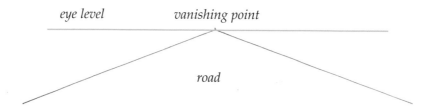

First find the eye level. To do this, hold a pencil horizontally at arm's length, level with your eyes. If you were standing in the middle of a road, as shown above, all the lines appear to converge to a single point called the **vanishing point**, although in reality they are parallel.

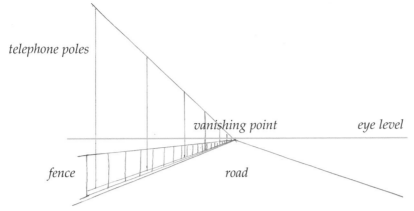

telephone poles

vanishing point

eye level

fence

road

To check whether a drawing's perspective is accurate or not, sketch in guidelines to the vanishing point. On parallel objects, horizontal lines converge to the same vanishing point. Here, guidelines have been drawn in to check that the fence and telephone poles all continue to the same vanishing point.

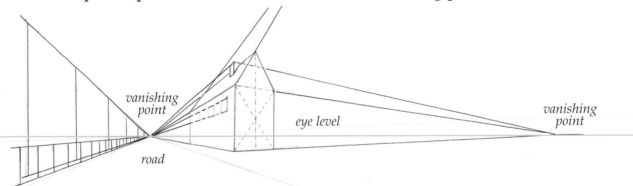

vanishing point

eye level

vanishing point

road

The house above has two vanishing points. The lines at the front go to the same vanishing point as the road, but those on the side go to a new vanishing point, as they are angled in a different direction.

TOP TIP

Using photos or magazine pictures, try to find the eye level and vanishing points.

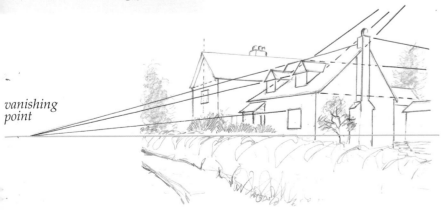

vanishing point

CHECK IT OUT

Always check that **proportions** and perspective are correct. Consider all the **elements** together to avoid mistakes. Here, dotted lines have been added to both houses to check that the lines follow the lines of the buildings.

TONE, TEXTURE, AND COLOR

One of the best ways of getting to know your materials is to practice making marks. Like handwriting, the way you draw will be unique to you. Experimenting with the tone, texture, and color of marks will allow you to expand the range of techniques you can use when drawing.

PENCIL HOLDS

When you are drawing, vary your hold on the pencil according to the marks you wish to create. See the four examples below.

1

To create long, pale marks, hold the top of the pencil and work with movements from the wrist.

2

To make shorter, darker marks, move your grip down the pencil toward the tip slightly.

3

To achieve very short, dark marks, hold the pencil close to the point and draw from the knuckles.

4

You can make broad marks by holding the pencil on its side. Vary your grip to change the tone.

A

B

TONAL VALUE

Tonal value describes the degree of darkness that a mark has. Being aware of tonal values will help you to create **contrast** between dark and lighter areas in a drawing. If you want to make a picture stand out more, it is better to add more tone to the darker areas, increasing the contrast. In these sketches of a window, image B has more tonal value in the shadows. This gives it more contrast.

Watercolor paper	Sketching paper

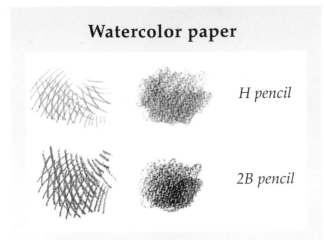

H pencil

2B pencil

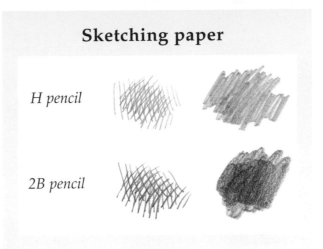

H pencil

2B pencil

TEXTURE

Marks and texture vary greatly depending on the materials that you use. These marks (above) were made using an H pencil and a 2B pencil on watercolor and sketching paper. The differences between the examples show the importance of trying out materials to see what type of effect they will create before you start to draw.

COLOR

Experiment with color pencils to see how the three primary colors—red, blue, and yellow—can be mixed to create secondary colors. In this color wheel, three shades of primary color have been used to create secondary colors.

secondary color

secondary color

secondary color

TOP TIP

To create grays, blacks, and browns, you need to mix all three primary colors together.

Draw your own wheel to start your own experiments. Try mixing the other shades of primary colors together to see what happens. For example, mix light blue with each of the three shades of yellow to make different shades of green. You can vary the amounts of each color by varying the pressure on the pencil to make more shades.

TONE, TEXTURE, AND COLOR

COMPOSITION

Life drawings can be the starting point for a more detailed study with a colorful background—something that may not have been present when the initial sketches were done. The careful selection of extra elements means that sometimes a more satisfying **composition** can be created.

CAT STILL LIFE

This cat has been sketched in a lovely pose, but it can be brought to life by adding other elements to add interest and color. In this case, these are a potted plant and a bowl of fruit.

STEP 1

The first step is to make rough sketches of each element on scrap paper so they can be moved around in relation to each other to find the most pleasing combination. It is important to plan carefully and take time at this stage to achieve a balanced picture.

STEP 2

Next, sketch out the elements together in a rough **outline**. Then choose a suitable color and begin to work up the shapes and outlines in more detail. Use gray for the cat, olive green for the plant, and orange, yellow, and ocher for the fruit. Then, starting with the base shade, add color on color to develop the shadows and highlights.

TECHNIQUE

STEP 3

The drawing should now be taking on more color and shape. Develop the cat's fur by varying the depth of color, and work up the dark areas with soft black. Purple shades can be used to unify the different elements of the composition. Shade the plant's pot and the plums, enrich the cat's fur, and add shadows.

STEP 4

Use different colors to complete the fruit, starting with base shades and overlaying with various shades to give the fruit texture and pattern. Varying the pressure of the color pencils will help to give elements a rounded structure. For example, you could vary the tones on the bananas (see left) to give them **form**.

Final image

Complete the composition by adding finer details with a very sharp black pencil. Add the shape of the cat's eyes, the whiskers, and fine hairs. Sketch in fine lines around the fruit bowl. By using the same shades throughout, it will help to unify the elements, making a balanced composition.

WATER AND SKY

Water and skies have long been favorite subjects for artists. They either form the main focus of a picture or provide an interesting background. The sky in particular can do a lot to set the mood of a drawing, creating atmosphere and drama, or simply a quiet, relaxing backdrop.

WATER

When drawing water, it is important to remember that it is a transparent substance, so you will be sketching reflections and movement rather than the water itself. When drawing still water, the rule is that the majority of marks will be horizontal, since the surface of the water is flat. When water is moving, such as in a river or waterfall, this rule can be ignored.

For calm water, the simplest way of creating a sense of movement is to add ripples. The aim is not to record every ripple you see. Instead, you can give a sense of movement by first creating a **wash**, then using a putty eraser to add horizontal highlights.

To create rings on the surface of the water, use horizontal marks in an oval shape. This is called the "ellipse effect." Make fatter marks on the sides, and long, thin ones at the top and bottom.

lines made with a putty eraser

Reflections are lighter, mirror images of objects. There are two main techniques. For moving water, create ripple-shaped marks with a darker tonal value. For still water (right), sketch in a perfect mirror image, then use a putty eraser to lift out horizontal lines from the reflection to suggest the surface of the water.

TECHNIQUE

SKY

A well-drawn sky can give a sense of space and depth to a picture. It can also help to create atmosphere—the dark, gloomy chill of a winter's day, or the bright warmth of summer. But how do you capture something that is changing by the second? Like any drawing technique, it is best to practice, experimenting with different materials until you find what works best for you. As a guide, always work with a soft pencil, which is easier to blend and is less likely to leave hard lines. For stormy, heavy skies, charcoal is ideal.

The simplest way to draw sky is to add a wash using a soft pencil, then blend to get rid of any lines. For paler skies, use a soft pencil and a light touch. Remove the pencil in cloud shapes with a putty eraser (right).

Give a drawing a great sense of space by making it mostly sky (left). Cirrus clouds have been created here by using a putty eraser to lighten wispy areas from a simple wash of gray.

You can give heavier cumulus clouds shape by adding shadows to them. Layering them gives a sense of distance and depth to the picture.

FLOWERS

Flowers are often added to drawings and paintings as they give color and life to a picture. One of the most important things to remember when drawing flowers is that they are complex, living forms, and no two are the same. Study them closely, but remember that you do not have to sketch every minute detail.

SUNFLOWER

The sunflower is such a cheerful-looking flower. Its bright, yellow color conjures up sunshine and summer days, making it a popular choice for artists to sketch. Study it closely before you start drawing, to familiarize yourself with its array of textures, from the smooth leaves to the rough center of the seed head.

STEP 1

Starting from the center of the seed head, sketch the letter "C." Add two rings to outline the darker center and the outer edge of the head.

STEP 2

Start to sketch in the outline of the top layer of petals. Try to ensure that you represent their different sizes and shapes, and the directions in which they lie.

STEP 3

Continue around the flower head, adding the remaining "whole" petals to the top layer. Note that gaps have been left for petals to be added on the underneath layers.

STEP 4

Start to fill in the spaces around the head with more petals. Be sure to overlap them in layers or your flower will look very flat. Then sketch in the basic outline of the stem.

veins

STEP 5

Next draw the outlines of the leaves, and sketch in the veins. You do not have to be completely accurate with this. Just follow the lines roughly.

17

TOP TIP

For all drawings, use an HB, B, or 2B pencil in the first stages so that any unwanted lines can be easily erased.

To create a shaded image

Work up the darkest tones in the seed head, smudging a highlighted ring around the center. Be sure to build plenty of texture into the seed head, to represent its rough, uneven surface. Develop shadow areas on the petals, leaves, and stem.

DAFFODILS

Groups of flowers make lovely compositions, as their varying proportions, colors, and shapes add interest to a drawing. In some ways, the daffodil is an easier subject than the sunflower because it has fewer petals and they are a regular size and shape. However, because the flower's trumpet stands out from the center of the flower head, you need to spend some time getting the angles right.

STEP 1

Begin by sketching the trumpet. Add the stamen inside and the outline of the trumpet's sides.

stamen

STEP 2

Complete the outline of the trumpet. Then sketch in the top petal and the center lines of the other petals. Make sure they are pointing in the right directions.

STEP 3

Next, sketch in the outlines for the remaining petals, taking care to sketch in lines where the undersides are visible on the curled petals.

TOP TIP

Many plants have petals and leaves that curl showing both sides. You can show this by using darker shading on the undersides.

FLORA AND FAUNA

STEP 4

Now sketch in the outline of the stem, and follow steps 1 to 4 to draw the other daffodil. Note that the lower petals of the left flower slightly overlap the flower on the right.

STEP 5

Finally, outline the simple shapes of the leaves. Where parts of leaves go behind the flower, sketch these in lightly so that you can check that each leaf emerges from above the flower head in the right place.

shading

highlights

To create a shaded image

Work up the shading on the trumpets and petals of the flowers, adding plenty of shadow where the trumpets join the petals. Now work up the leaves, shading the undersides of the folding leaves darker. Add highlights to the petals, leaves, and trumpets with a putty eraser. Finally, use a sharp pencil to add finer details.

BIRDS

Animals are great subjects, and birds are particularly interesting, thanks to the varied and wonderful color and texture of their feathers. As with any animal, it is a good idea to take plenty of photos and use them to work from as your subject is sure to change position or even fly away!

DUCK

A duck is a good bird to choose as your first subject. They are fairly common, so finding one to sketch should be easy. Like many birds, the male of the species has brighter feathers. By choosing a male you will be able to add plenty of tonal variation to your picture.

STEP 1

Start by drawing a large, oval shape and a small oval shape at an angle for the basic positions of the duck's body and head. Join the two together with a rectangular shape for the neck.

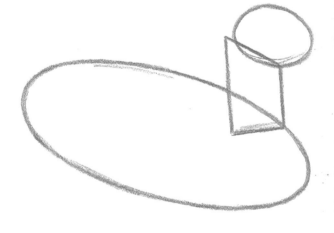

STEP 2

Draw a rectangular shape on the front of the head to represent the beak. Sketch in a large triangular shape to mark the wing position, and add a smaller triangle for the tail.

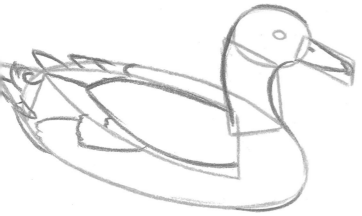

STEP 3

Now that you have the basic shapes, start to refine the outline. Sketch in the outline of the beak and the curve of the neck, as shown. Add detail by sketching in the outlines of the tail feathers.

STEP 4

Add a pale wash to the duck. Build up the darker areas by adding shading to the back of the head and neck and the front of the body. Be sure to follow the curve of the body. Add curved and **hatched** shading to the wing and tail to suggest layers of feathers. Shade the darkest areas of the tail to add contrast.

TOP TIPS

When you are sketching feathers, check that your shading lines follow the direction of growth. Varying the lengths of the feathers will also help them look more realistic.

To create a shaded image

Shade in the eye and finer details on the beak. Then use a putty eraser to add highlights to the head, neck, and body. Do not forget to add a highlight to the eye as well. Finally, add some movement lines around the front of the body to suggest ripples in the water.

OWL

The owl often crops up in art as a symbol of wisdom. Drawing owls will give you a chance to practice sketching complex patterns and different textures, from their downy chest feathers to stiff, long wings and tail feathers. Unlike ducks, owls are harder to see in the wild, so work from photos or visit a bird sanctuary.

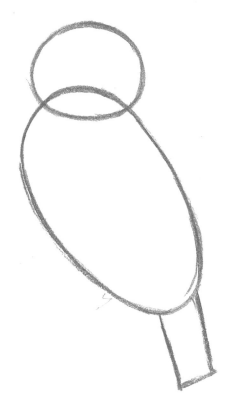

STEP 1

As with the duck, start with a large oval for the body. Overlap this with a circle for the head. Add a rectangle for the tail.

STEP 2

Now sketch in the shape of the wing, extending the tip onto the tail area. Draw in the facial features. The large eyes fall just above the central line of the face. Sketch in a small "v" for the beak and a heart-shaped outline above the eyes.

STEP 3

Next, sketch in the outline of the neck. Then add the basic outlines of the post and the owl's feet.

STEP 4

Now use a soft pencil to add a gray wash to the owl. Use long strokes to create the feathers around the eyes and on the tail and wing tip. Then define the dark area around the beak. For the feathers on the wing, draw "v" shapes. Use shorter strokes for the fluffy chest feathers. Create some circular patterns on the chest, then smudge them. Finish the outline of the owl's feet.

To create a shaded image

Fill in the eyes. Add shading to the feet, then use a sharp pencil to define the claws and add definition to the beak and around the eyes. Create highlights on the eyes, face, wing, and chest area. Finally, add some shading to the wooden post.

CATS

The cat is a very popular subject. If you do not have one, it is likely that you know someone who does, so you will have plenty of opportunities to do quick sketches and take photos before you start your drawing. If you are familiar with your animal subject, you can really capture their personality.

SITTING CAT

In this drawing, the cat is shown in a familiar sitting pose. If you want to sketch a pet, you would be advised to take photos to refer to, in case your subject decides to move mid-sketch!

STEP 1

To start, sketch the basic shape of the body. For this cat's sitting position, you need to draw the back and chest areas as circular shapes.

STEP 2

Now, add a circle for the face. Sketch in the shape of the cat's tail and the outline of the legs.

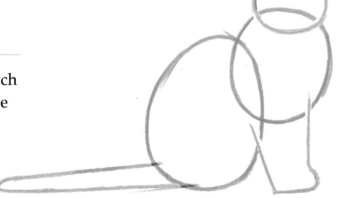

STEP 3

Add triangular shapes for the ears. Draw a line from the cat's head to its back to create the shoulder and nape of the neck. Do the same to connect the back and tail. Now outline the back feet and sketch in the front legs and paws in more detail.

STEP 4

Sketch in the eyes, the triangular shape of the nose, and the inverted "y" shape of the mouth. Add a few whiskers, too. Use your pencil to add short, feathery lines to the back to soften the fur. Work up the tonal structure with shading marks.

TOP TIP

Give the eyes more depth by varying the pressure on the pencil as you shade them.

To create a shaded image

Add a pale gray wash. Then shade the darkest parts of the fur, blending lines so they look natural. Note that the curve of the cat's hip needs to be shaded in and shadows added to the legs and tail. Begin to work up the finer details, concentrating on the ears and the eyes, and adding highlights with your eraser as the final touch.

TABBY CAT

The complex markings of a tabby cat look daunting, but remember that you do not need to reproduce every one—it is enough to follow their general outline. Spend time looking at the tonal variations on your subject, as this will help you to give the cat form and roundness.

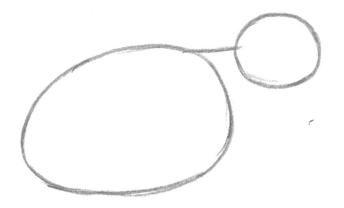

STEP 1

Start by drawing a large oval for the body. Then draw a smaller one for the head, joined to the body by a line to indicate the back.

STEP 2

Now sketch in the basic outline of the ears, chest, and legs. Since the cat is looking away from us, the line of the back of the head seems to continue almost vertically from the ear to the chest. Sketch the outline of the top of the tail curled around the body.

STEP 3

Add the facial features: the eyes, the "t" of the nose, and the inverted "y" of the mouth. Draw in lines for the whiskers and some of the darker marks of the head. Sketch a couple of lines under the chin to show folding where the cat's head is turned. Lightly sketch in the tail markings.

STEP 4

Work on the outline of the back of the head and the chest area, and draw and shade darker areas of the tabby's markings.

Create a shaded image

Add a gray wash, then use a sharp pencil to add finer detail. Outline the eyes and define the whiskers. Add some short strokes to the cat's back and tail to give the fur more texture. Build the shading between the tail and body, and between the front legs. Use your putty eraser to add some highlights under the jaw and on the tail and face.

DOGS

Dogs, like cats, are probably one of the easiest subjects to find. There are a number of basic rules to follow with proportion, and you will need to adjust these depending on the breed and age of the dog you are planning to draw.

PUPPY

The proportions of any baby animal are very different to those of an adult. This puppy has a large head in relation to its body. It also has short legs and very large paws, which give it a cute, yet slightly comical appeal. The front-on pose suggests that it is curious and ready to play.

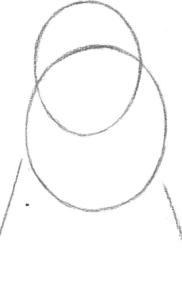

STEP 1

Start by sketching the puppy's basic outline, with oval shapes for the head and body. Outline its position with a trapezoid—the legs can be sketched in later.

STEP 2

Add large triangles for the ears—they are more than two-thirds of the length of the head. Now sketch in the shape of the legs. Draw a horizontal line between the front legs to mark where the back feet will fall. Sketch in guidelines for the back legs.

STEP 3

Now that you have the basic shape, you can start to work on the outline of the legs. Draw in circular shapes for the paws—remember that these are large in proportion to the puppy's body. Make sure that you sketch in the curve of the knees as well.

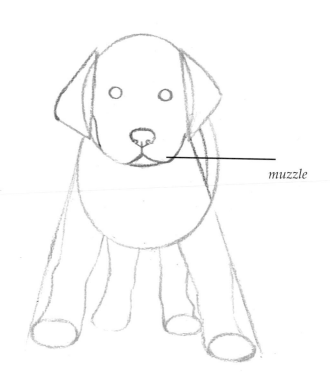

muzzle

STEP 4

Add in the facial features. The eyes are set almost halfway down the head. Draw in the outline of the nose and mouth, and the shape of the muzzle and chin. Add a line on each side to outline the puppy's sides.

To create a shaded image

Start with a light gray wash, then build up shading to develop the fur using short strokes and following the general direction of growth. Use a softer pencil to build up the darkest tones, paying particular attention to the eyes, the cheeks, chest, back legs, and paws. Use a putty eraser to add highlights to the brow, nose, ears, and chest, as well as the front paws.

DALMATIAN

The long, elegant form of this Dalmatian is very different to the short, rounded shape of the puppy on the previous page. The side-on view emphasizes its lean shape. Although it may appear that this is simply a black-and-white drawing, in fact, there is a lot of tonal variation needed.

STEP 1

Start with two ovals for the body—a smaller one for the rump and a larger one for the torso. Sketch in a rectangular shape for the neck and an oval for the head.

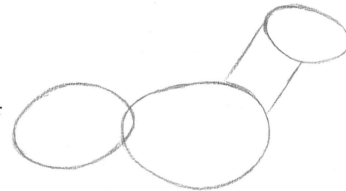

STEP 2

Now sketch in the basic position of the legs. The legs are long and elegant. Remember that a dog's back legs have reversed knee joints.

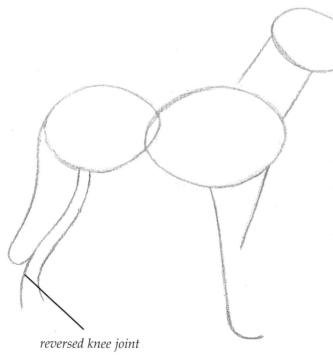

reversed knee joint

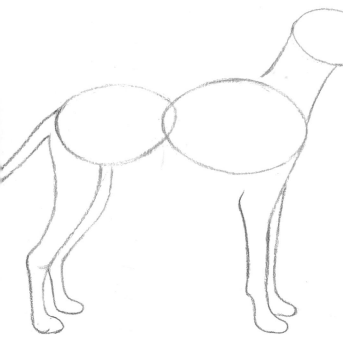

STEP 3

Work on the outline of the tail and legs, sketching in more shape. Notice that the paws are more in proportion than those sketched for the puppy.

STEP 4

Draw in the ears, and work on the outline of the face, giving the nose a slightly upturned end. Add shading to give form to the neck, legs, and ears, being sure to work up the shadow on the legs at the back of the picture. Sketch in some markings all over.

Create a shaded image

Once you are happy with the overall shape, continue to work on the shading to add definition to the face and body. Make sure that you blend the lines to avoid any hard edges. Finish the markings by building up the layers of black so that they stand out. Shade the eyes and add definition to the paws to complete your drawing.

HORSES

Horses may appear to be a complicated subject for the budding artist, but all it takes is time to study them to understand their shape and proportions. Get to know how they stand and move to make your drawings more realistic.

STANDING HORSE

This standing pose is an ideal one to start with. But the reality of drawing any animal is that they are unlikely to pose for long. Looking closely at your subject will result not only in a better sketch, but will also improve your observational skills!

STEP 1

The basic shapes for the horse are very similar to the dog (see p. 30). Draw an oval for the face, adding a circle inside. Sketch a large oval for the body, and an overlapping circle for the rump. Connect these to the head with a triangular shape for the neck.

STEP 2

Now add more detail with circles for the mouth and cheek and triangles for the ears. Sketch in the tops of the legs and the knee joints. Draw in the outline of the tail, and sketch in the curve of the neck.

STEP 3

Add in the mane, eye, nostrils, and cheekbone. Refine the shape of the head and body, sketching in the curve of the back and the tops of the legs. Add the basic shape of the lower legs, ankles, and hooves. Thicken the tail, adding some movement.

STEP 4

Now concentrate on refining the shapes and angles. In particular, begin to draw in the mane in more detail and sketch in lines to represent the muscles. This will help to define your sketch giving the horse more of a three-dimensional feel.

Create a shaded image

Add a light wash, then gradually build shading to create definition. Note that the mane and the lower legs have been left fairly pale. Use a putty eraser to add highlights to the rear and front legs. Finally, add finer detail to the face and mane with a sharp pencil. Add dark shading to the nostril, outline the eye, and add wisps of hair to the mane and tail.

JUMPING HORSE

When horses are moving—especially galloping or jumping—their muscles are long and taut, so you need to use heavier lines. Watch horses in motion to see how their movements change at different speeds. Getting their anatomy right will make your drawing more realistic.

STEP 1

As with the standing horse, start sketching the basic shapes of the head, neck, shoulder, torso, and rear. Note that the rear of a moving horse is angled because the legs are thrown out behind the horse as it leaps forwards.

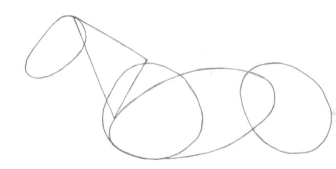

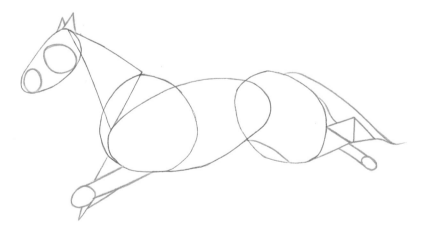

STEP 2

Add the basic shapes for the top of the legs, from the body to the knees. The left front leg leads, and the back legs are thrown out almost parallel to each other. Sketch in the shape of the ears, the cheek, and the mouth, and add the tail shape.

TOP TIP

Spend time getting the positions of the legs right.
This will make your drawing more realistic.

FLORA AND FAUNA

STEP 3

Add in the lower legs and hooves. Then refine the outline to make the horse look more rounded. Curve the back to show that it is stretched, and define the tops of the legs. Sketch in the eye, nostril, and cheekbone. Add the suggestion of the mane along the back of the neck.

STEP 4

Use long strokes to define the muscles to show that they are stretched. Add plenty of lines to the head and torso. You can also begin to show more detail on the tail, sketching in long hair lines.

Create a shaded image

Add a pale wash over the horse's body, then work up the areas in shadow. Pay particular attention to the neck where it joins the back, and the underside of the legs. Use your putty eraser to add highlights. Work up the finer details of the mouth and eyes. Finally, use sharp lines to define the muscles.

LEPRECHAUNS

With magical creatures, such as leprechauns, you can use your imagination to bring a picture to life. In folklore, the leprechaun is a mischievous male fairy, usually shown in the form of an old man wearing a green or a red coat.

LEPRECHAUN

According to folklore, leprechauns hide their treasure at the end of a rainbow. If captured, they must reveal their pot of gold to their captor. Do a drawing of this little fellow looking as though he has just been discovered, his arm curled protectively around his gold!

STEP 1

Start with the basic outline. Emphasize his small stature by making his head large for his body. The head is an egg shape. Sketch in the feet and the shape of his left arm.

STEP 2

Continue to outline the shape of his legs, adding detail to his shoes. Add in the shape of his raised right arm. You can also add guidelines for his bushy beard and the brim of his hat.

STEP 3

Continue putting in the details on the leprechaun's body, adding the hem of his shorts and the outline of his belt and hat band. Now outline the pot.

STEP 4

Add in the outline of the rainbow as well as the leprechaun's pointed ears and facial features. A very long, pointed nose gives him a slightly comical air. Sketch in his heavy moustache, and add the belt buckle and heel lines to his shoes.

STEP 5

Add more details to his face, sketching in heavy eyebrows, apple cheeks, and pupils in his eyes. Start to work up the shape of his bushy beard with a wavy outline. Sketch in the coins, and define the curve of his legs, adding two small lines on top of his shorts to suggest the shape of his knees.

STEP 6

Use a sharp pencil or pen to draw over the outline. The rainbow has not been outlined because the colors tend to merge slightly. Shade the drawing using color pencils. Make sure to work darker shades into areas of shadow for greater contrast.

FAIRIES

For centuries, humans have told stories about fairies. There are many legends about these tiny creatures, some of whom were believed to be kind, while others are mischievous. When drawing fairies, try to bring out their magical, playful natures and let your imagination go wild!

SINGING FAIRY

This light-hearted **cartoon** of a fairy singing as she plays the guitar is fun to draw. You do not need too much of a background. However, since fairies tend to be associated with nature, you could add a hint of grass and some flowers. The bright purple and yellows work well together, but you can choose any colors to finish your drawing.

STEP 1

Start by sketching the basic shape with a circle for the head, a triangular shape for the body, ovals for the wings, simple stick legs, and circles for the feet.

end of the guitar

STEP 2

Add triangular shapes for the ears, the outline of the headband, and curling tail shapes for her hair. Outline the body of the guitar, then sketch in the curve of her right arm and her hand. Sketch the end of the guitar as a simple circle to the right.

STEP 3

Sketch in her raised eyebrows and simple curves for the outline of her closed eyes. Her nose is shown by a small wavy line. Sketch the mouth as a line with a rounded end like a "6." Add curves underneath for her lips and chin. Add detail to the guitar, and sketch in her fingers and shorts.

STEP 4

Add simple patterns to her wings and top, varying the size of the circles. Sketch in details of her left hand—her thumb is on top of the guitar neck and fingers below. Sketch the detail on her shoes, and add a simple grassy background and two flowers.

STEP 5

Use a sharp pencil or pen to draw over the finished lines (right). Then use color pencils to shade in the picture. Since the drawing is a cartoon-style piece, the colors look solid, but you can still add shadows and areas of contrast using black hatching lines. To show that the fairy is moving, add a couple of lines around the wings and legs. Finally, shade in the grass and flowers.

FLYING FAIRY

This flying fairy is drawn in a more realistic style. Her proportions and features are more human than the singing fairy. Understanding proportions and how the human body moves will help you to sketch a realistic pose. Notice that her back is arched and her feet are raised behind and above her.

STEP 1

Sketch the round head and a long, curved body. Sketch in an oval for the hips, then the outline of the legs and feet. Add circles for the knee and ankle joints. Make sure her feet and legs are raised high, as if she is diving. Now sketch in the shoulder joints, arms, and hands, as well as the elbow and wrist joints.

TOP TIP

Many art shops sell desk-top mannequins, which can be used to help you plan and sketch different poses.

STEP 2

Sketch in the basic wing shapes, the outline of her flowing hair, and her chest. Draw a vertical line to mark the center of her face. Add three horizontal lines as guidelines for the positions of the eyes, nose, and lips. The eyeline is just above center.

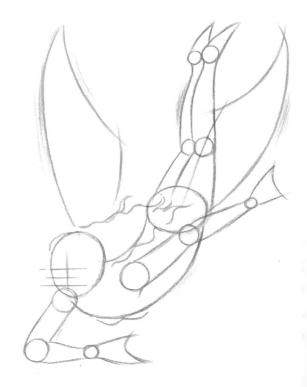

STEP 3

Make sure you are happy with the pose, then add the wing patterns. Add the straps of her dress, the ribbons trailing around her arms, and a leaf tucked behind her right ear.

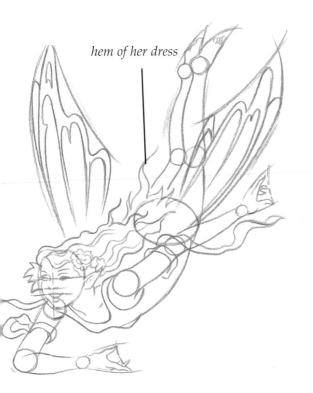

hem of her dress

STEP 4

Add the facial features—almond-shaped eyes, eyebrows, nose, and smiling mouth. Add more lines to her hair to give it texture, and draw in the rose tucked behind her left ear. Outline the jagged edge of her hem, and draw her fingers and toes.

Create a shaded image

Add a wash, then add shadows to give form. Notice the line of the left leg has been left visible under the translucent wing. Use hatching lines and movement lines around the fairy to suggest that she is flying. Use a sharp pencil to outline the fairy and add detail. Use a putty eraser to add highlights.

DRAGONS

Dragons are featured in many legends. In Asia, the dragon is a powerful, magical symbol, whereas in Western culture, the dragon is feared. Folklore tells of many different types of dragons—some are winged, others are serpent-like.

FIRE-BREATHING DRAGON

This dramatic close-up of a fire-breathing dragon is an exercise in using your imagination. In some ways this can give you freedom, but you must make sure that your sketch still has form and the proportions are correct. Look closely at pictures of dragons in books and on the Internet to see how other artists have brought realism to this mythical creature.

STEP 1

Sketch a large oval for the head, and two ovals for the neck. Draw a circle inside the head shape to mark out the basic outline of the open mouth. Mark the positions of the ear and horns using triangles to give the basic shapes.

STEP 2

Draw in triangles for the eye, the lower lip, and nostril. Sketch half a circle inside the mouth area to mark where the far side of the mouth will be. Now sketch out the basic shape of the neck frills, or spines, on both sides of the neck.

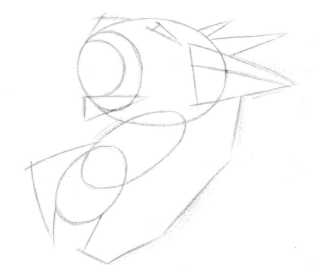

STEP 3

Continue adding elements to the mouth:
the teeth, a curling tongue, the bottom lip,
and the wattle (the frill under the chin).
Add the neck frills, and sketch in the line
of the backbone with spines.

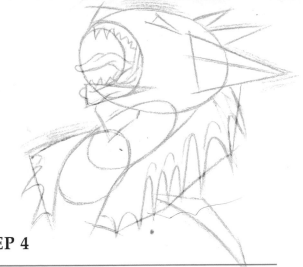

STEP 4

Add the curve of the nostrils, the heavy
eyelid, brow ridge, and the flowing hair
around the face. Work up the wattle and
neck frills, sketching in lines to show
the spines. Add some flame shapes to
the left to show fire coming out of the
dragon's mouth.

STEP 5

Use a soft pencil sharpened to a point
to outline the dragon's body. Add details
to the eye, drawing in a vertical pupil.
Start to sketch the hair around the face
in detail, and add small circular marks
to the neck, back, and frills for the scales.

Create a shaded image

Add more shading to give your dragon
form. Use hatching lines on the neck, face,
ears, and frills for the darker areas. Add
shadows to the horns, teeth, the underside
of the tongue, and inside of the mouth.
Finally, smudge in some highlights on
the scales and frills and on the head.

DRAGON ON A ROCK

This dramatic drawing of a fierce dragon, perched high on a rock is really impressive. The pose, with wings outstretched and the tail curled around the rock, suggests that the dragon is about to take off. It is peering into the distance—perhaps it is about to swoop down on some unsuspecting prey!

STEP 1

First, sketch in the basic shape of the wings and the main part of the body. Add the shape of the head. Notice that it is lower than the body.

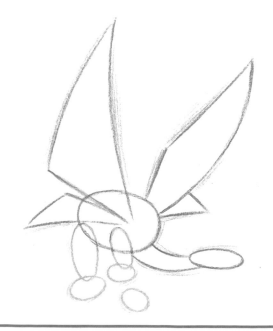

STEP 2

Sketch in the outline of the neck, curving downwards as the dragon looks intently at the ground below. Add the bottom part of the wings as smaller triangles.

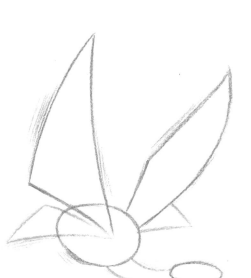

STEP 3

Add the back and front legs, sketching the feet separately. Dragons are usually drawn with small, short front legs, so make these narrower and smaller than the back legs. Sketch in a circle for the left back leg below the right front leg.

STEP 4

Start to give the wings more shape using curves and spines. Add parallel hatching lines to give the wings form. Sketch in the tail curving around the rock. Continue the shape behind the rock as a dotted line to help you line up the two parts of the tail. Give the tip of the tail a tight curve to make it look as if it is flicking impatiently.

STEP 5

Now add a wattle, spines, and hair flowing around the face. Continue the spines onto the tail, adding a feathery tip. Sketch in the details of the feet, adding pointed claws to the toes. To suggest that the tail is moving, add some loose stones falling off the rock.

Create a shaded image

Outline the dragon and add a light wash, then work up the darker areas. Add scales on the wings. Use a putty eraser to add some highlights on the tail and wings. Finally, add a darker wash to the rock, and use hatching lines to give it form.

SOME FAMOUS ARTISTS

Throughout history, there have been some truly great artists who were masters at drawing. You may have heard of them, or seen their work in books or at an exhibition. But it would be wrong just to see them as people who draw. Many produced sketches to plan great paintings, and these initial ideas are seen today as works of art in themselves. Learning more about these artists and their techniques will help you to improve your own drawing skills.

LEONARDO DA VINCI (1452–1519)

As well as being a mathematician, scientist, inventor, musician, and writer, the Italian "Renaissance man" Leonardo da Vinci is considered to be one of the greatest artists of all time.

Although he is best known for his paintings—the most famous being *The Mona Lisa* and *The Last Supper*—few have survived. However, the large collection of drawings and sketches that remain show how wide his interests were, from sketching flying machines to anatomical drawings, the most famous being *Vitruvian Man* (right).

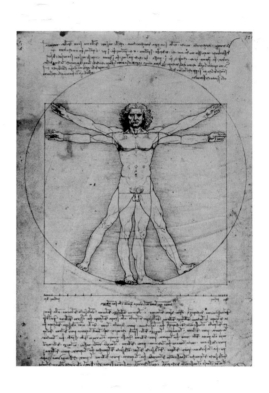

MICHELANGELO (1475–1564)

Michelangelo was another great Italian Renaissance artist who was often a rival of Da Vinci. He is also celebrated as one of the greatest masters the world has known.

Michelangelo was an exceptional sculptor, painter, draftsman, and architect. His best-known works are the frescoes he painted on the ceiling of the Sistine Chapel in the Vatican in Rome, and his statue of David in Florence, Italy. He also left behind a huge collection of drawings, including his *Anatomy Sketches* (left).

EDGAR DEGAS (1834–1917)

French artist Edgar Degas was one of the founding artists of the Impressionist movement in Paris.

Degas' many sketches of dancers, such as *Seated Dancer* (left), are perhaps some of his most well-known works. His extensive studies enabled him to master form and pose in a way that many other artists never achieve. In fact, although he also practiced photography, he often went back to sketching to capture dancers, as he was able to draw them so quickly and accurately. Degas' sketches and portraits were also notable for their psychological complexity and their depiction of human isolation—qualities which show even in this relatively simple study.

M. C. ESCHER (1898–1972)

Dutch artist Maurits Cornelis Escher is known for his architectural drawings of impossible realities and constructions.

Escher's drawings have a strong mathematical influence, and many experiment with symmetry and impossible objects. Some of his most famous works are *Waterfall*, which appears to flow both up and down, *Ascending and Descending,* and *Drawing Hands* (right).

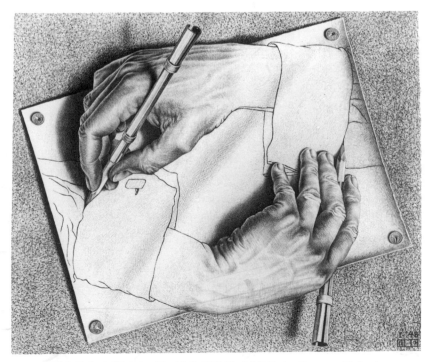

M.C. Escher's "Drawing Hands" © 2009 The M.C. Escher Company-Holland. All rights reserved. www.mcescher.com

SOME FAMOUS ARTISTS

GLOSSARY

blend To soften and mix, mostly used to describe how parts of a drawing are smudged to ensure no hard lines remain

cartoon A style of humorous sketch or drawing

composition How parts of a picture are arranged together to make a whole image

contrast Opposing colors, forms, or lines placed close to each other for intense effect

depth A richness or intensity of color that creates the idea of dimension

elements The different things that make up a picture

fixative Spray used on drawings done in pencil, charcoal, Conté, chalk, or pastels to keep them from smudging

form The shape of something

hatching Lines drawn close together to give an object shape

highlights An area or spot on a drawing, painting, or photograph that appears very bright

outline The line marking the outer shape

perspective The way that objects in the distance look smaller and blurry

proportion The relative size of one thing compared to another

putty eraser A soft eraser that can be molded to a point, making it useful for rubbing out very small areas on pictures

shading Adding darker tones to create shape

sketchbook A pad of thick, textured paper

smudge To smear or blur the edges

stump A pointed roll of paper used to soften lines

subject The thing or person that you are drawing

texture Using shading, space, line, and color to show how an object would feel if you touched it

tonal value The relative darkness or lightness of a mark made in drawing

vanishing point The point at which all parallel lines in a drawing appear to meet

wash A light layer of color spread over an area of the paper

INDEX

A

ancient
  Egyptians 4
  Greeks 4
  Romans 4
animals
  birds 20–23
  cats 12–13, 24–27
  dogs 28–31
  horses 32–35
  puppy 28–29
artists
  Da Vinci 5, 46
  Degas 5, 47
  Escher 47
  Goya 5
  Kandinsky 5
  Klee 5
  Michelangelo 5, 46
  Monet 8
  Raphael 5

B

birds 20–23
  duck 20
  owl 22

C

cartoon-style 38
cave paintings 4
colors
  primary 11
  secondary 11
  wheel 11
composition 12, 13, 18
contrast 10, 21, 37

D

depth 5, 13, 15

E

ellipse effect 14
eye level 8, 9

F

flowers 16–19
  daffodils 18–19
  sunflowers 16–17
frescoes 4, 5, 46

H

highlights 7, 12, 14, 21, 23,
  25, 27, 29, 33, 35, 41, 45
horizon 8

M

magical creatures
  dragons 42–45
  fairies 38–41
  leprechauns 36–37
materials
  charcoal 7, 15
  cotton swabs 7
  craft knife 7
  ink eraser 7
  paper 6
  pencils 6
  putty eraser 7
  sandpaper 7
  spray fixative 7
  sticky notes 7
  stump 7
  wedge eraser 7
movement lines 14, 21, 33,
  39, 41

O

observation 8

P

papyrus 5
pencil holds 10
perspective 8, 9
proportions 9, 28, 31, 40, 42

R

reflection 14
Renaissance 5

S

shading
  curved 18, 19, 21, 23,
    25, 27, 31, 43
  hatching 21, 39, 41,
    43, 45
sky 14, 15

T

texture 10, 11, 13, 16,
  17, 27
tonal value 10, 20, 25,
  26, 30
tone 10

V

vanishing points 8, 9

W

wash 15, 21, 23, 25, 27, 29,
  33, 35, 41, 45
water 14